Jonathan Ferrier

alpha beasts

Pointless Poems for Frustrated Fauna

Illustrated by Matt Rowe

Mereo Books

1A The Wool Market Dyer Street Cirencester Gloucestershire GL7 2PR
An imprint of Memoirs Publishing www.mereobooks.com

alphabeasts: 978-1-86151-540-7

First published in Great Britain in 2015
by Mereo Books, an imprint of Memoirs Publishing

The address for Memoirs Publishing Group Limited can be found at www.memoirspublishing.com

The Memoirs Publishing Group Ltd Reg. No. 7834348

The Memoirs Publishing Group supports both The Forest Stewardship Council® (FSC®) and the
PEFC® leading international forest-certification organisations. Our books carrying both the FSC
label and the PEFC® and are printed on FSC®-certified paper. FSC® is the only
forest-certification scheme supported by the leading environmental organisations including
Greenpeace. Our paper procurement policy can be found at
www.memoirspublishing.com/environment

by Wiltshire Associates Publisher Services Ltd. Printed and bound in Great Britain by
Printondemand-Worldwide, Peterborough PE2 6XD

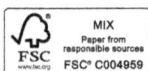

MIX
Paper from
responsible sources
FSC
www.fsc.org   FSC® C004959

PEFC
PEFC/16-33-415

Foreword

I confess that this book is written primarily to amuse – for the amusement of myself and other humans, (particularly those who enjoy contact with their fellow species).

However, if it has any theme at all, it is that other animals also have feelings and even aspirations. They are not here just for the benefit, and exploitation of humankind.

JFF – October 2015

Axolotl

Have you seen my axolotl,
Bursting with verve and vim and bottle?

I'm afraid that not a lot'll
Have seen an axolotl.

For of course he's very rare,
Must be treated with great care.
A lake in Mexico's his home,
But now it's drained, his home has gone!

The Billy Goat

There's nothing nice to say of note,
About your friend the smelly goat.
His temper's bad, his bite is worse,
And as for gardens, he's a curse.
(I can think of nothing sillier
than munching on my bougainvillea).
He eats all things that can be chewed
And has a dreadful attitude.
My walls, he climbs, however hilly,
At best he's just a Silly Billy.

The Crocodile

Some men accuse the crocodile
Of being a reptile full of guile.
It's sad he's so misunderstood,
His aim in life is to be good.

His eyes brim o'er with tears of sorrow,
Because he knows that on the morrow
He'll have to find some beast to eat,
And then they'll talk of more deceit;
Those people who walk down the street,
And go to shops to buy their meat!

A Dog

Yes, I'm a dog!
That's what I am;
So please don't call me "Little Lamb".
My Mistress says I'm mostly good,
And I agree that so she should.

I'm good with kids and dogs and smells,
And loads of other things as well.
But best of all, I'm good at food,
(I know that food don't rhyme with good,
But pers'nally I think it should.)

You see I'm just a Labrador,
And that's what Labradors are for,
Cleaning up plates and ee'n the floor.
"Aren't you full up?" Let me assure
You, that I always can eat more.

The Elephant

The Elephant is large and grey,
And looks as if he's here to stay,
You'd think he would be very slow
But show him bees and watch him go.

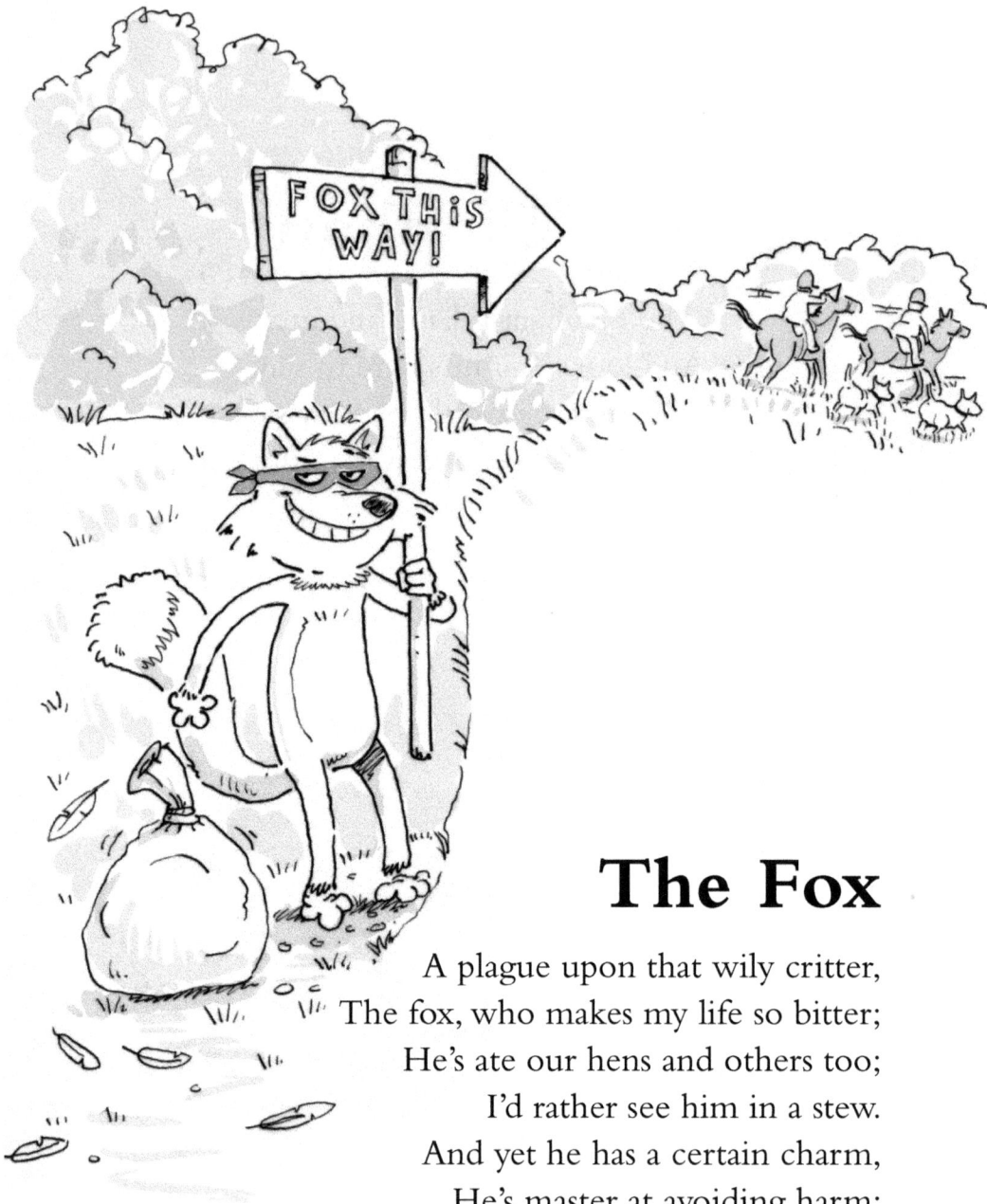

The Fox

A plague upon that wily critter,
The fox, who makes my life so bitter;
He's ate our hens and others too;
I'd rather see him in a stew.
And yet he has a certain charm,
He's master at avoiding harm;
His brazen cheek and slippery cunning,
Earn some respect, not hunts and running.

Frog

Hoppety-hip, I'll go for a dip;
Splashety-splosh, I like a nice wash;
Stonkety-stink, not water you'd drink;
Bongerty-bog, it's fine for a frog!

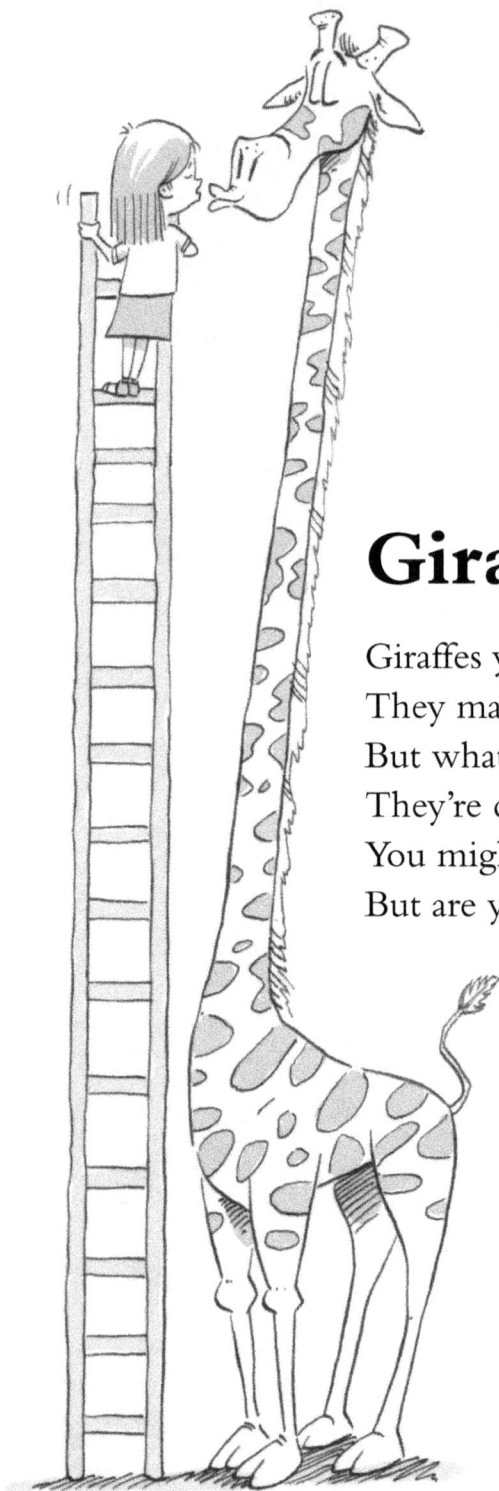

Giraffes

Giraffes you know are very tall,
They make the rest of us feel small,
But what they really want is this,
They're desperate for a tiny kiss.
You might not think that's much to ask,
But are you equal to the task?

The Hippopotamus

A naturally enquiring mind
Is just the thing you'd hope to find
In Hippos, for a simple grunt
Is not sufficient at the front
To balance such a vast behind.

The Ibex

Do not tease the Alpine Ibex,
He's a cultured sort of beast.
Ask yourself this question, "Why vex
One not fearsome in the least?"

Yodelaaaaay-He-Hooo!

Sound of Music is his passion,
Yearns to yodel o'er the piste;
Musicals are out of fashion,
But his longing's never ceased.

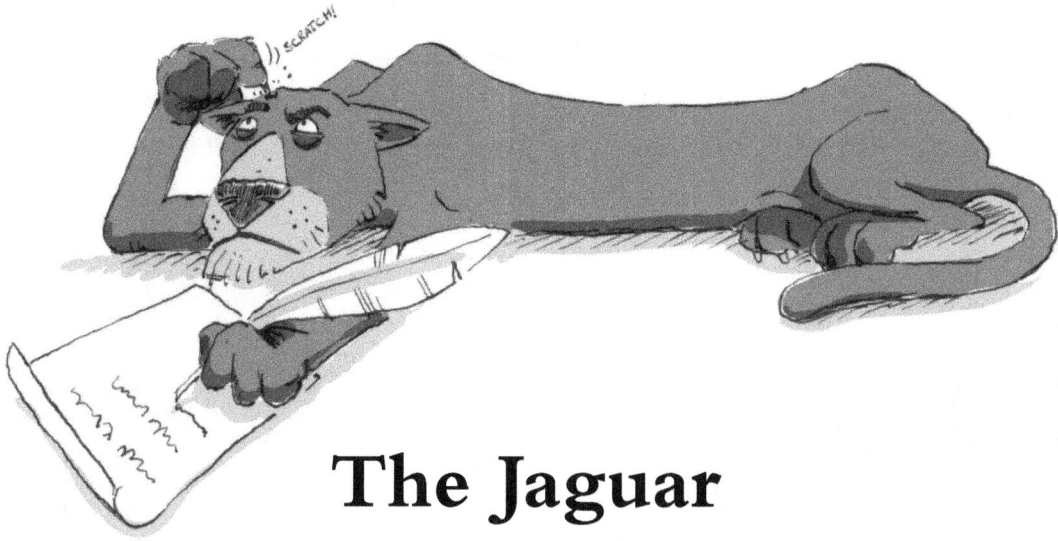

The Jaguar

Sleek and black, and fleet of foot,
The jaguar would never put
His name to a mere motor car
He out performs such toys by far.

He's so adept at catching prey,
He could spend hours asleep all day;
But he prefers to use his time
Creating epic verse in rhyme.

Kangaroo

Some Aussie's hate a kangaroo,
And I'll admit, I might do too.
On modern roads this hairy hopper
Is liable to come a cropper;
It waits until a car is on it ,
Then bouncing on the screen and bonnet
It skips off to the neighbouring bush,
And leaves your car a nasty mush.

The Lion

You must resist the urge to spy on
That king of beasts, the froshus lion,
For underneath his bold outside
He has a dreadful fear to hide;
He's terrified of being seen
As soft and sweet, not fierce and mean,
Tho' really he would so much rather
Eat lettuce leaves, than chew your father.

Mice

We have no time for Mister Burns,
Who wrote of mice in dreadful terms;
"Wee sleekit, cow'rin tim'rous beastie"
Does not describe us in the leastie.

AHEM!

It's not from fear, but finer feelings
Make us avoid cat's double dealings;
If we don't choose to make a bee-line,
For that deceitful creepy feline.

Although we mice are small in stature,
That can't obscure our noble nature;
Honest, bold, and free from vice,
There's no species half as nice.

The Newt

It must be made completely clear,
The newt's repute is most unfair.
He is the model of sobriety
In amphibious society.

Frogs and toads will often deviate
From sober paths, become inebriate;
Newts abstain from all that drinking,
They excel at abstract thinking.

The Orangutan

That sweet, benign orangutan
Is hatching up a master plan.
He shelters under leaves from rain,
While fiendish plots form in his brain.

He plans to ask humans to tea,
But behind bars, so they can see
What he feels like when in a zoo
And people gawp if he's in view.

The Pig

The portly pig is kind but shrewd.
Although she ponders most on food,
Her thoughts can turn to higher spheres,
'Life's meaning' churns between her ears,
And 'Does true love cause endless tears?'

The Quagga

You will never see the Quagga,
  Gallop o'er the great Karoo,
Nor e'en saunter with a swagger
  Round a paddock at the zoo.
They were hunted to extinction
  For their meat as you can see,
The last one in a known location
  Died in eighteen eighty-three.

The Rat

I used to know a supercilious rat,
Who was polite but didn't hold with chat.
He had a bold and patronising air,
And wore a hat to hide his greying hair.

A bit aloof, he really didn't care
What people thought, or if they'd stop and stare.
My wife disliked his manner, and that's that;
She introduced him to our neighbour's cat!

The Snail

Do not rail against the snail,
Or throw him o'er your neighbour's fence;
That's not his destructive trail;
Killing him can make no sense.

It's that thug the slimy slug,
Who's been eating all your plants.
Give your snail a gentle hug;
He will sing Gregorian chants.

Tiger

Tiger, tiger, sleeping tight,
Give the tourists quite a sight.
Eating one would be a sin,
Tho' better than not being seen.

Sit up, stretch and give a yawn,
Must be up, it's after dawn.
Each immortal pic. or frame
Helps a bit to save your name.

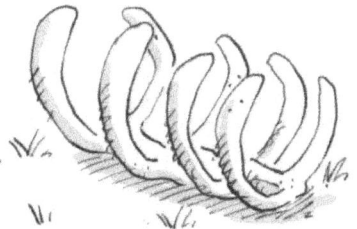

Unicorn

I have to say the unicorn
Treats other beasts with utmost scorn.
He's noble, Yes; but oh so haughty;
His attitude is very naughty.
Some people think he can't exist,
And frankly he will not be missed.

Vipers

On safari through the jungle,
You might feel you've made a bungle,
If you get a viper's bite.

They at night will sleep in bed
And by day avoid your tread,
Very shy stay out of sight.

If your leg a viper's bitten,
By pangs of guilt he would be smitten,
Couldn't sleep a wink all night.

The Worm

Do not harm the humble worm,
Pull his tail and watch him squirm.

Do not feed him to the fish,
Would you wish to be their dish?

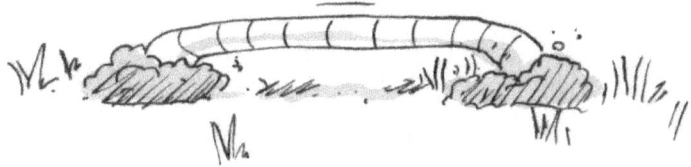

He can be a loyal friend,
Love you always, end to end.

X-The Cross Child

X marks the spot where that cross child
Raged against his parents mild,
Rolled on the floor and screamed and stamped,
Bellowed in unreasoned rant.

Not allowed more sweets today;
Couldn't get his selfish way;
Tried to use a deafening wail
To gain his whim through loud blackmail.

The young of other beasts behave,
Only children rant and rave.
Is this what makes the human race
Lay claim to take Earth's highest place?

Yak

Hiking in the Himalayas,
You may hear your Sherpa say as
How he cannot lift your pack.

For you're taking far too much,
Food, tents, stoves, ice-picks and such,
Can't be carried on his back.

He will ask that woolly wonder,
Trudging upwards, to far yonder,
He'll enlist the helpful yak.

The Zebra

The zebra's problem is his name,
It winds him up inside;
Should it be Zee, should it be Zeb,
He really can't decide.

Acknowledgements

Many friends and family have been supportive and encouraging, and I am very grateful to them all, because I always need encouragement to finish the job. However three people in particular have acted as editors, giving valuable criticisms and suggestions for lines that don't scan or are too clumsy; they are two retired English teachers, Robert Sanderson and Caroline Cochrane, and my daughter, Susan. (I have not always taken their advice and so lines that still don't work, are my own fault).

As always my publisher, Tony Tingle has been invaluable both in producing the final design and layout, and in giving me large amounts of advice on everything from the books themselves, to marketing, publicity and my website.

Above all I am indebted to Matt Rowe, not only for his witty and characterful drawings, but for his ability to make them enhance the poems.